ANIMALS AND FISH

Jill Sherman

Enslow Publishing
101 W. 23rd Street
Suite 240
New York, NY 10011
USA
enslow.com

WORDS TO KNOW

beeswax A wax that bees make. It is used to make candles and furniture polish.

down The fine, soft feathers of some birds.

insulate To keep heat in.

manure Fertilizer made from animal poop.

natural resource Something from nature that people use.

renewable Able to be replenished.

CONTENTS

Living Resources

Earth is our home. It is also home for animals. But animals and fish are also natural resources. We need animals for all kinds of things!

Fast Fact

Bees do an important job. They move pollen from flower to flower. This makes fruits and other crops grow.

What's for Dinner?

People need to eat. And animals are a great food. We raise chicken and cows on farms. We hunt for ducks and deer. We catch fish from rivers and oceans. Their meat makes a healthy meal.

FAST FACT
Animal resources are renewable. There can always be more of them made.

More Food from Animals

What else comes from animals? Chickens lay the eggs you have for breakfast. That glass of milk came from a cow. Even the cheese on your pizza came from an animal.

Hide and Hair

We also use animals to make clothes. Their hides make leather. It is sewn into coats and shoes. Animal wool is spun into yarn. Wool sweaters and socks keep us warm.

FAST FACT
Silkworms make a thin fiber that people weave into silk fabric.

Keeping Us Warm

On cold winter days, you need a warm coat. Animals have fur. It insulates their bodies. Birds have soft feathers called down. Coats with fur and down are very warm.

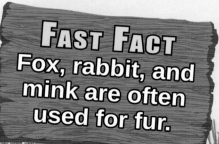

FAST FACT
Fox, rabbit, and mink are often used for fur.

Animals in Our Products

Animals are hiding in many products. Crayons can contain animal fat. Beeswax candles can light your birthday cake. Natural sponges come right from the sea.

FAST FACT
You might not think poop is worth much. But animal manure helps plants grow.

Animals at Work

Animals do work to help people. Mules carry heavy loads. Pigeons carry messages. And dogs sniff for unsafe materials, such as guns.

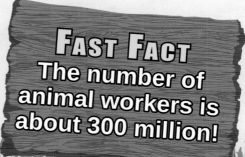

FAST FACT
The number of animal workers is about 300 million!

Safety First

New products need to be safe for people. So companies first try them on animals. We learn a lot about humans this way.

FAST FACT
Mice, rats, and rabbits are often used to test products.

Smart Fishing

Fishermen pull in loads of fish. But not too many! Some need to stay in the sea. They will be there when we need fish later. They make more fish, too.

FAST FACT
Healthy fish and animals are good for the environment.

Activity

Animal Product Hunt

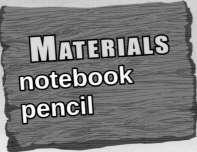

MATERIALS
notebook
pencil

Procedure:

1. Go on an animal product hunt! Search your home for products made from animals. Start your hunt in the kitchen. Make a list of every product you find in that room.

2. Make a new list and hunt for products in your bedroom. Write every product down.

3. Continue searching. Make a new list for each room.

4. Which room had the most animal products? Which had the fewest? What do these products have in common?

LEARN MORE

Books

Prior, Jennifer Overend. *Our Natural Resources*. Huntington Beach, CA: Teacher Created Materials, 2014.

Yashuda, Anita. *Explore Natural Resources: With 25 Great Projects*. White River Junction, VT: Nomad Press, 2014.

Websites

4-H Club
4-h.org
Learn about this national organization that teaches young people about animals and the environment.

US Fish and Wildlife Service
fws.gov / refuges / kids
Read animal facts and play games.

INDEX

Published in 2018 by Enslow Publishing, LLC.
101 W. 23rd Street, Suite 240, New York, NY 10011

Copyright © 2018 by Enslow Publishing, LLC.

Library of Congress Cataloging-in-Publication Data

Names: Sherman, Jill, author.
Title: Animals and fish / Jill Sherman.
Description: New York : Enslow Publishing, 2018. | Series: Let's learn about natural resources | Includes bibliographical references and index. |
Identifiers: LCCN 2017011012| ISBN 9780766093850 (pbk.) | ISBN 9780766093867 (6 pack) | ISBN 9780766092389 (library bound)
Subjects: LCSH: Zoology, Economic—Juvenile literature.
Classification: LCC SF84.33 .S54 2018 | DDC 591.6/3—dc23

LC record available at https://lccn.loc.gov/2017011012

Printed in China

Photo Credits: Cover, p. 1 Georgette Douwma/Photographer's Choice/Getty Images; pp. 2, 3 stockphoto-graf; interior pages (soil, grass, sky) Andrey_Kuzmin/Shutterstock.com; interior pages (sign) johavel/Shutterstock.com; p. 4 Alin Brotea/Shutterstock.com; p. 6 clearviewstock/Shutterstock.com; p. 8 thieury/Shutterstock.com; p. 10 unverdorben jr/Shutterstock.com; p. 12 MaeManee/Shutterstock.com; p. 14 Yellow Cat/Shutterstock.com; p. 16 KellyNelson/shutterstock.com; p. 18 Mirko Sobotta/Shutterstock.com; p. 20 jordache/Shutterstock.com.